Listen Up

Listen Up

Listen Up

A Memoir of Perspective

Fred Duncan with Sabin Duncan

Fielding Books

Listen Up

Published by Fielding Books
© 2016 Sabin Prentis Duncan

ISBN - 13: 978-0-9984885-0-9
ISBN - 10: 099848850X

All rights reserved
First Printing

Fielding Books
PO Box 74191
Richmond, VA 23236
www.sabinprentis.com

DEDICATIONS

To my co-pilot, Joanne Duncan, it seems like yesterday we were agreeing on how we were going to raise these boys. Then we did that and much more than we imagined.

To my sons, Damon & Sabin, you may think that the father to son thing is a one-way relationship. It's not. I learned from you while I was at it. I was also inspired to do my best because of you.

To my grandchildren, siblings, extended family, and friends, with you, I aimed to be a trustworthy and reliable person. I hope you can see those intentions beyond any human shortcomings.

- Fred

To my parents, Fred & Joanne Duncan, I appreciate how you cultivated a love for words within me. Now it's my turn to reciprocate and I do so with an abundance of love.

- Sabin

OTHER TITLES FROM FIELDING BOOKS

Fiction
Assuming Hurts by Sabin Prentis

Non-fiction
Reflections from the Frontline by Sabin Duncan

Fred Duncan

Table of Heart Matters

Listen Up

Politics

Faith

"You know the family is the solution

to the world's problems today

Now let's take a look at the family

In the family the father is like the head,

the leader, the director

Not domineering, but showing love, guidance

For everyone else in the family

Now if we could get all the fathers of the world

To stand up and be fathers

That would be great."

- Kenny Gamble & Leon Huff
Family Reunion
performed by The O'Jays

What kind of book is this?

Listen Up is borne from the sentiment of giving someone their flowers while they can smell them. Beyond sentiment, *Listen Up* is tangible evidence that an everyday, working man can develop remarkable sons. My brother, Damon, is a transformative leader in urban development. Peoples' lives are enriched as a result of Damon's work. To see Damon is to see a manifestation of the sacrifice and commitment of our father, an everyday, working man. Then there is me. As an educator, I have also had the fortune of enriching people's lives. Whether in a kindergarten classroom, as an elementary school principal, or a professor / administrator at a HBCU (Historically Black College & University), I have had the great fortune of enhancing hundreds of lives. Like Damon's, my work is an outgrowth of the sacrifice and commitment of our father everyday, working man.

How does an electrician from Ford Motor Company touch the future? He does it by serving as the fertile soil from which his children and grandchildren can grow. He does it through more than 50 years of marriage, modeling for black boys how to respect and treat a Black Woman. He does it by pushing, instilling, and supporting his boys toward an understanding that the world was bigger than his circumstance. He does it with love.

As a book, *Listen Up* does not have a precedent. It is a unique collaboration between a father and a son. A collaboration that extends my father's wisdom beyond his limited time on Earth. It is a flower of a book that was given to an everyday, working man while he could still smell it ☺ .

Prologue

Listen Up

The eagerness of a five-year old effervescent with the knowledge that their Show-N-Tell presentation would be the best is a snapshot of my feelings in presenting the following insights, reflections, and words of wisdom from my father, Fred Duncan.

Many of my fondest childhood memories are connected to our home in Northwest Detroit. Off the top of my head, there were maybe twenty something young men and boys who lived along our street - my best buddy, Lenny; his big brother, Sean, Quan, Boom-O, Ced, Lil' Lawrence, Stanky, Leon, Mark, Clarence, Morris, Lorenzo, Lucky, Lil' Charley, Bud, Junior, Reg, Shooby, Cool Bryant and his younger brothers - Mark, Stacey, & Damon, along with Nate, Potsie, Eli, and lil' EJ. With a collection of boys like that, it was easy to get a game of street football or backyard basketball going. However, among those nostalgic recollections, there is one uneasy truth: less than half of those boys lived with their father. Neither then nor now, did I ever view this with any type of pity. Instead, then, like now, I was eager to share what was the best Show-N-Tell on our street, my dad.

My larger than life perceptions of my father are embodied by his 6'5" height. What is even more sentimental is that my dad would occasionally join me and the other boys in backyard basketball. With our youthful exuberance, we would attempt to run around him, shoot quick jumpers before he could block them, and annoyingly try to swipe the ball from him. All of our efforts would be in vain. What was not in vain was my dad's methodical sky hook shot - the patented shot of the NBA's leading scorer, Kareem Abdul-Jabbar. With both hands on the ball, he would take a large step with his left foot, raise his right knee really high, then fully extend his right arm with the ball resting on his fingertips, and with a flick of the wrist propel the basketball into the net - *Swish*. Every time - *Swish*. Out of everyone's reach - *Swish*. Methodical - *Swish*. Reliable - *Swish*.

Just like his role as a father and husband, my father's skyhook was a bundle of mundane factors that resulted in desired outcomes. Enduring marriage; *Swish*. Raising sons in a tumultuous environment; *Swish*. Evolving as a human and spiritual being; *Swish*. Modeling "A way" instead pontificating about "The way" - *Swish, Swish, Swish*.

I could continue; but beyond the value of my memories is the value of the wisdom he shares. Lately, my dad has been using Facebook to bestow his sapience. With *Listen Up*, I aim to share a number of his most poignant posts. In those posts, one can gain a perspective of a man who has lived, learned, and loved. Moreover, one can glean ideas that can help with their own skyhook shot over life's adversities. Because as my dad would often ask, "The ball (life) is in your hands, what are you going to do with it?"

~ *Sabin*

Note to Reader
The following pages are written in Fred's speaking voice. The written word cannot convey the nuance of his tone, pitch, and facial expressions. To know Fred is to be accustomed to understated humor, metaphoric meaning, and self-depreciating modesty. He describes his writing in the following way:

"I beg forgiveness of my English teachers, as one might think that I only walked past the classroom, rather than attended, but that was long ago."

By all means, continue reading and soon you will become accustomed to "hearing" Fred's unique voice.

Fred Duncan

Family

Listen Up

Maturity grants perspective. As a husband and father, I have a greater perspective of the man my father is. I now more greatly empathize with the challenges he faced and the perseverance and faith it took for him to proceed. In a book co-authored with my dad, it would be easy to assume that my feelings for him are all rosy and idealistic. They are not. As a man, my father experienced life's ups and downs just as all of us do. But as an exceptional father, he was man enough to be self-revealing and honest with me and my brother. In a sense, he would place his shortcomings on the table and dissect his thought processes and areas he could have better handled situations so that we could be better men.

Damon and I have an inside joke that whenever Dad leads in with "The old boy was thinking …," when he moves himself to the third person, that's our cue that he is going to share a nugget of important introspection. However, all joking aside, we appreciate his ability and willingness to be vulnerable with us, reflect with us, and teach us.

Of all the valuable lessons he shared, he modeled the most important lesson of all: his role in the stability, success, and functioning of our family. Before we knew Fred, the man; we were loved, protected, and guided by Fred, the father. It's no wonder that Damon and I equate fatherhood with coolness; we learned from the one of the coolest fathers of all.

~ *Sabin*

Joanne

All too often, my wife and I laud our sons without acknowledging each other, which would leave the wrong impression. My wife since 1964 has been an essential component, in our sons' success as well as the success of our marriage. God saw fit to bless our struggles with the boys. Putting our children through school was the mantra, from the inception. That common goal *righted* the good ship Duncan on many occasion as we pressed thru waves of opposition and challenge, common to most young folks starting from scratch. She found her calling early as a RN (registered nurse), of which I'm proud. We had our ups and downs as I endeavored to complete college (but never did). We were confronted by and overcame the unmentionable *power struggle* that ensues if the wife out-earns the husband. Thank God for the boys. I felt that their well-being and foundation outweighed me *getting my hat* (leaving). I'm sure she often felt the same; after all, she was a professional, brains, cute face, and great legs. I felt that I was the shit and certainly more intelligent than I am now at almost seventy-three. One problem, we had that misunderstanding between two fools: we loved each other. So let the wind blow and the waves of tribulation break across the bow, the good ship Duncan seeks the horizon already populated with great grandchildren. For the Creator has kept us, when we could not, and at times would not have kept ourselves. Gotta' go now, there's a big grin with a sagging diaper here, demanding the Admiral's immediate attention.

A Visit from his grandson, David

No one told me how special you were going to be. You began with just an ordinary grey hue that later succumbed to gold. It was just another day. Your coy beginning hid your gift for me. My grandson was at the door, "What's up granddad?" preceded a bone crushing hug. "Boy, sit down." David endured my raw juice concoction as I fumbled out a breakfast. We had a couple of hours of that time old guys cherish, time with the grandkids. The conversation went from this to that, and back to this. The topics flew and settled on responsibility, relations, man, both Black and White, God, Black and White, and beyond. While in my listening, I glimpsed his mother's face and my son's likeness as well, and somewhere deep inside smiled. Later as he and his little family rushed to their flight, I thought of how my day had been embellished by their light. Sometime later, after night had crept-in, he texted their safe arrival. Therefore I submit, my offering of gratitude to the Creator, as tonight, my heart is at ease and my head rests on a pillow of peace.

One Morning with my grandson, Ryan

Had a police encounter this morning. My grandson's Jeep gasped to a stop right in front of the police station on the main thoroughfare through Ypsilanti, Michigan. Traffic immediately backed up exponentially. Unable to restart it, Ryan called AAA. Before they got there, we needed to move the truck. His slight framed body seemed too light for the task, while my 6ft.plus, 228lb. only looked adequate. I didn't dare challenge my impaired lungs for fear of passing out, even though I had my oxygen working, I knew the work was beyond my impaired capacity.

Thankfully, a policeman rushed to our assistance. Without hesitation or passing judgment, the policeman handily pushed the Jeep off Michigan Ave. into a parking lot, and as only an officer would, into a parking space. We thanked him as he hastily made his way back into the building - my gratitude for today.

Nostalgia & the World Series

I am not a baseball fan, but my dad loved every aspect of baseball, from the spitting of tobacco to the butt-scratching, and stalling before his windup that preceded him firing an aspirin-like missile at my cheap baseball glove. "Boy, baseball is a man's game; it'll make you tough!"

The toughest thing was enduring Van Patrick's fawning over the Tigers for two and a half hours. This World Series has changed all that, and all I can say is, "Wow! What strategy, what pitching, what a tension-filled series!" I still can't stand chewing tobacco, but I am enjoying this series. I miss Fred (Sr.) and the occasional sip of his Pabst Blue Ribbon, which was always followed by a warning of 'Boy, don't tell your mama." We would have enjoyed this series, and the beer would have been on me. Love you, dad!

Thankfulness

Today, I'm thankful as my children have traveled both near and far and returned safely, and also for the people in my life that have the empathy to be of assistance in life's trying times. I hope to never become so jaded by good fortune that I am not grateful for the Creator's blessings. "Save it be the grace of God, there goes I." That paraphrase of a bible verse came to mind as I observed the weather related hardships that have beset our neighbors in Louisiana and California. How very fragile our comfort zones can be. How temporal, when a lifetime of work and accumulations be lost in a matter of minutes. Aside from the ongoing debates on the bible, and personage of a Savior, I'll issue my thanks, before the tempest rages.

Fred Duncan

Race

Listen Up

I started a new school in seventh grade and the school year commenced with three half-days. The fourth school day, which was a Monday, was our first full day. But more notable than that, just four days into the school year, there was a scheduled meeting between my teachers and my dad.

The teachers' concerns stemmed from my homeroom teacher's disbelief that I would speak my truth. During the first hour on the first day of school, our teacher gave us the first of her numerous intimidating lectures. She was indeed a character, straight from the children's stories-mean-teacher-casting center. While she was attempting to indoctrinate us to her rules, I became more attentive to whatever was going on outside the window. Amid her welcoming harangue, she stopped at my desk and asked, "Am I boring you?"

Surprised, I looked at her and around at my new classmates. Then without malice or sarcasm, looked her in the eye and replied, "Yes."

I had not yet been a student at the school for sixty minutes and I was already put out of class.

In what has become a reality for too many Black children, I was subjected to the bigoted biases of an opinionated, presumptive teacher. Her attempt to label or categorize me was annulled by my father that following Monday afternoon. Yet, perhaps more than his vigilance for preserving my growing identity, it is within the nexus of experiences with that teacher and the after-school conversations with my dad that serves as the rich soil in which my understanding of racism is rooted.

One day, I was sharing how the teacher seemed significantly enamored with Napoleon Bonaparte. She shared stories, facts, and perspectives with a gushing enthusiasm that would match pre-teen girls meeting members of a popular boy band. As I recanted her stories of Napoleon, which I should add were impressive to me in the way young learners are shaped to idolize George Washington or Alexander the Great. My dad was nonplussed. While I am paraphrasing, I remember my dad's response like this: "Yeah, Napoleon was alright, but that greatest emperor stuff is bullshit. He ain't got nothing on Hannibal."

Prior to that conversation, I had never heard of Hannibal. Imagine the awe of a 12-year old who was infatuated with G.I. Joe, when he learned about a military leader who led a couple thousand warriors to Rome on elephants. My mind was blown. My dad also dismissed the history books' approach of taking our shit and probably depicting Hannibal with European features. To make a long story short, my father never disregarded Napoleon. He disregarded the notion that European history is world history. He disabused the notion that all the cool shit was happening in Europe while Africans and everyone else was just waiting to be guided in the European way.

While I can imagine that he figured it would happen, my dad had empowered me to raise my hand during the next Napoleon-is-the-greatest diatribe and inquire about Hannibal. Unlike the first day of school, my tone was laced with sarcasm and malice. But just like that first day, I was put out of class. Except, there was no ensuing conference with my dad; that teacher had already had her Waterloo and knew my dad was not buying that bullshit.

~ *Sabin*

Racial is not Racist

Racial is not racist. I may be alone in this, but my first response to the court house murders in western Michigan was, "Man, I hope he wasn't Black"-that is racial, but it's not racist. I was disgusted by "Precious" an abundantly "melinated" sister in a blond wig - racial, not racist. The plethora of Black contestants on Springer, Maury and that irk that populate non-primetime TV, in their too short dresses and their airborne wigs representing all Blacks (covertly); I'm appalled but those depictions are racial, not racist. The media's parade of the Detroit Public School's unprincipled principals who took bribes and stole the school children's money for themselves; while the very same media deliberately shields the images of the White vendor who was making major bucks off that miscarriage of ethics - racial for White interest, but racist to me. What does all that say to our children, who may only notice the parade of the un-principals? Finally my point, racial to me could be seen as racist to a White person, while racist to me may simply be seen as racial to them. After four hundred years of "bad press," forgive my lack of an olive branch with the media aided boot of oppression still on my neck. My reply may seem racist, but it's racial to me.

Patriotic Hypocrisy

With all the uproar about the dissension of Colin Kaepernick and the hypocrisy it unveiled, what has been a longstanding right of Americans and one of the precepts of our "national pride" has caused the bigotry that pervades too many of our brethren to fester into blind rage.

There's a stain on the robe that in which Americans clothe themselves, deposited by racial injustices from long ago. Although we may declare God from the majestic mountains to the idyllic towns and hamlets, that stain won't wash out. You have paycheck protecting Blacks cowering behind a "patriotism" that never said a word about the murderer at Mother Emanuel setting fire to the hallowed flag. Nor were the hyper-patriotic Whites outraged at his overt disdain for Old Glory. Yet the media, the real culprit in this drama has remained mum on that matter. I say that because one only has to take note of the increased viewership generated for Colin's next game.

The real game is as trite as it is repulsive-Let's you and him fight, while I reap the spoils. The red meat of injustice is flung into the streets of race conscious America and the "it" (profits) hits the fan. We are being played folks. Like a cheap guitar.

What's On Your Mind?

I'm almost humored by the Facebook request of, "What's on your mind?" While retaining a degree of sanity, my response is as follows: There is not an issue more pressing than innocent citizens murdered by those sworn to be their protectors. The fragile guise of accountability disintegrates whenever a group is asked to police themselves. Lame excuses such as "I had my body camera turned off" or "The hood was up on the patrol car at the critical time of an alleged crime" are unprofessional. Are we fighting crime with crime? Who made those key components options, in the first place? Was it our deified judicial system? Could it be their antiquated dispensation of justice to the poor and non-whites is mired in a bygone era when the robes of justice were white sheets? No robe is so white that it can purify wrong, nor one so black that it can hide injustice. No grand jury should be so unaccountable that it can trample the public trust as though it was some child stomping a mud puddle. Justice is looking the other way while minions of murder play judge, jury, and executioner with the public trust, and the lives of the disenfranchised.

There are men and women of honor in uniform; as evident by our community's grief for the family of one recently lost. He was a protector, a cop's cop, and a representative of those brave enough to tackle wrong. The public has an obligation to those unheralded, underpaid protectors of the peace, just as they're mandated to call out those that have brought dishonor to the profession.

American Paradox

There is a profound dilemma prowling this land of the free and home of the brave. The dark hand of denial has vilified one of America's subjects for exercising his constitutional right to dissent. Something about him being unpatriotic, acting all non-black, and making all that money. As we wade deeper into the mire a more glaring paradox surfaces, the corpses of the protected citizenry who have been gunned down by their supposed protectors. Again the deeds are not congruent with the words. Lawd have mercy. Christianity may be the religion of the land, but that acclaimed mercy and justice are not the practice. Meanwhile, segments of the citizenry want to criminalize anyone who doesn't believe that fat meat is greasy. Could this be make believe? This thing called the court of public opinion or something more ominous like manufactured consent. The stench of a controlled media permeates the air. However, that's foray is for another day.

The redeeming quality in all this is that in America the platform for being free to voice your dissent remains precariously intact. Therefore hope has not abandoned the hopeful and where there is an ember of hope there is a chance that the flame of truth will eventually spring forth and light the pathway for just men to tread.

Fred Duncan

Our Great Country?

Too much lawlessness? Too much lying? Well, too much injustice then? No. Too much senseless murder. The disregard for human life across the spectrum of America is terrifying and utterly appalling. USA!? The media would have you believe that it's a Black thing, suggesting that America needs to do something about you people, masking the fact that non-Blacks are being marched to the graveyard in record numbers also. USA! USA? People shouldn't have to live, no, shouldn't have to die like this. Some would say that it's the times we live-in. What?! Road rage? Somebody "dissed" me? Driving While Black? Are these justifications? I beg your pardon. We should beg for a redefinition of this charade we have named, civilization. USA! USA? Even the descendants of the ice people (Dr. John Henrik Clarke) in Europe are not plagued by such bloodshed among themselves. With my hand over my heart, America is supposed to be the example, the epitome of Christianity, and every other 'anity and 'ism. After all, "God spread His love on thee." We have digressed. Is this how we thank a patient Creator? Arrogance, bloodshed, ingratitude all seem to be a fad. USA! USA? My plea is that we look to how great Thou are compared to how great we aren't. We need an appreciation of human life, rather than wanton bloodshed and the twerking butt cheeks of some misled woman, before the sweep of the pendulum completes its arc back into Jim Crow.

Others & Us

I am grateful for another Sunday. Daytime lumbers forth bringing promises of fellowship, unencumbered relaxation and at least one good meal. There are those that have adorned themselves in their Sunday-only finery, while others are re-glossing their four-wheeled pride for the Dream Cruise - a time to burn rubber on Woodward Avenue, if you so desire. As certain as the bread is on our tables, our culture is tied to the automobile here in Southeast Michigan.

As a matter of fact, it's an amalgamation of cultures that make up this auto culture; resulting in food you wouldn't normally eat, friends you wouldn't normally have, and even cuss words you wouldn't normally say. I've broken bread with a number of different races, shared tears, laughter, wine, and exotic offerings of unknown variety. Having had deep discussions with reverends, racist, rebels, and radicals - I have concluded that our similarities outweigh our differences. We all want a dignified life with provision for our families. Sarcastically brilliant of you Duncan, but why were some brothers, making the same money, working the same jobs, staying at the same economic stratum? Many of my Arab friends moved to this country, lived with their cousins' family and saved. Later, they would move their family in with their cousin's family and save their money. Only to later buy a store with his cousins, all watched over and advised by some older individuals shuffling about in the background of that modest enterprise. Some of my Black friends would condescendingly mock their apparel and mine too. Oh but a few years later, the business expanded and Abdul's Mercedes, that his kid had carelessly parked out front, signified the wisdom of his ways.

Then if we look to the barometer of American success, the White guy - he has a boat, a cabin, a home, a bike, a pickup, two cars, a partridge, and a pear tree. But that's how White guys roll, it's expected. The Indian doesn't work at the plant anymore; he can't afford the cut in pay. Moreover, his elders are still somewhere on the premises, perhaps in West Bloomfield. Oh, and the West Indian brother, he's doing just fine with property here and back home, still his taste in clothes could use a boost. But for some of those everyday Blacks I feel for the high degree of sadness for those once vociferous brothers that put down those of us who spent money on private school for the kids, getting the wife educated, and ignoring our own personal interest. Culture is an "us" institution and a culture's success depends on an "us" state of mind - not me, but "we" and that "we" that begins with family.

It's a beautiful day in the neighborhood.

Colin Kaepernick

Colin Kaepernick. Welcome, pull up a chair my brother. Joanne, can you get this fella a plate? Behold how easily we embrace one of our own. As your identity unfolds, you will find the soul of the Blacks, that heartfelt hug, ride or die, if you will. Not to be confused with better. We are just different. Pass the corn bread please. If you don't know it that is partly the reason we are in the situation we find ourselves today. It is a misconception that others want to be our friend just because we want to be theirs. History says otherwise. Most non-melinated people want the advantage rather than friendship, and at their best, an advantaged/friendship, where they are deemed more worthy in all aspects of life. By denying your heritage, you may be crowned their friend. Some Blacks have taken on the trappings of America's majority and have been handsomely rewarded; however, their lot is a dubious existence. Ask Bill Cosby. You are never too big to fail, or be felled. Would you like so more lemonade?

Colin, you hold hands with Jack Johnson, Ali, Malcolm, Fannie Lou Hamer, Sojourner and countless Blacks who have taken a stand against what is wrong and stood for what is right. Not what the flag represents, but what it misrepresents. Now some of the advantaged will curse you for it, as they cursed the zoo keepers in Harambe's (the gorilla) death. That unsaid statement: the value of the primate exceeded the value of the child. The aftermath of which resulted in an almost criminal investigation of the child's family. Duh. The implication, don't get grabbed by a gorilla if

34

you are Black. King Kong was just a movie, but had Fay Raye been Black, she most likely would have been accused of luring that naive monkey into harm's way with her seductive apparel. Did you get enough to eat? Again, I say welcome to our humble abode.

Which Reminds Me ...

In the ongoing narrative, Black is more of a state of mind than a skin color, I was pleasantly surprised to see more celebrities join in support of Black justice from law enforcement, particularly biracials, who are in a precarious position with both races - not Black enough to some, and not quite White to others. I sometimes think God has a sense of humor, because he can take a modest-looking interracial couple and literally "Hit it out the park" and give them absolutely beautiful children - sort of an "Up yours" to the racist of the world. Then to encounter that most melinated lady with a smile that has to be on loan from heaven, who astounds you with her age which may be twenty years more than you could possibly have imagined. Such is life. Now I'm old enough to recall those "If you're brown, stick around..." days, so to see more inclusion within the Black race, makes me hopeful. For acceptance is growth. One might say, "Black minds matter."

When was America Great?

"Once upon a time," those words brought warmth and joy into my distant childhood because they were a prelude to a fanciful journey that assured a happy outcome. I loved sometimes sitting on the teacher's lap as she read fairy tales. I relished those stories, even though they weren't real.

Later, I encountered new phrases like, "Keep Dearborn Clean," which meant no Blacks. Dearborn, Michigan had neither Black residents nor businesses, until after the Arabs came bearing fragrant vessels of that ultimate lubricant, money. Today, Dearborn looks better than before. Hear tell, there was a sighting of a Black man mowing his lawn, in Dearborn. "Let's Keep Dearborn Halel," if you will.

Currently, there is a new phrase afoot, "Make America Great Again." Sounds noble enough to me, except that, exactly when was America great? Perhaps they're referring to those postwar years when the economy was booming with new housing for the veterans and quality goods were manufactured here. Perhaps I missed that great time after my family had sojourned-up North, where racial bias wore gloves rather than the gnarled fingers of southern bigotry; yeah, perhaps that was the time. Better, but hardly great. Perhaps I should consider the source; and at this most critical juncture in America's political arena maybe we all should differentiate between reality and rhetoric, for the latter is only make-believe.

Fred Duncan

Photo Album

Listen Up

Fred Duncan, Sr.
Fred's father

Essie B. Duncan
Fred's mother

Lawrence Thompson
Fred's maternal grandfather

Ida Mae Thompson
Fred's maternal grandmother

Joanne Quince & Fred Duncan, Jr.
Spring 1963

Fred & Joanne's sons: Damon & Sabin
1977 (above) & 1983 (below)

Fred & Joanne Duncan
Summer 1989

Fred, Ramona, Sabin & Joanne
Summer 2001

Listen Up

Sabin, Fred, & Damon
Summer 2001

Ryan, Damon, Mary, Damon II, & Fred
Summer 2001

Fred & his siblings: Lee Edward, Essie Mae, & Harry
Fall 2005

Sabin & Fred Duncan
Fall 2008

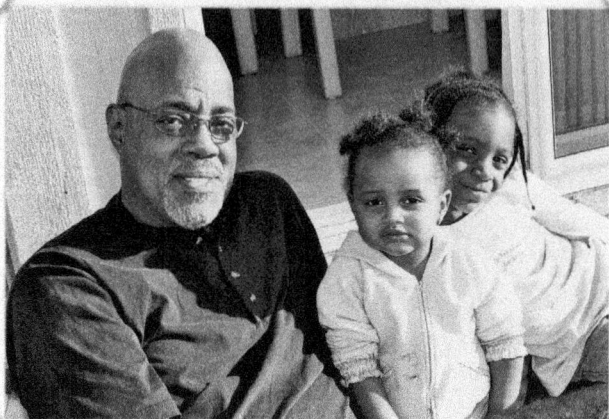

Fred & his granddaughters
Seylon & Sanaa ~ Summer 2008
Dominique ~ Fall 2011

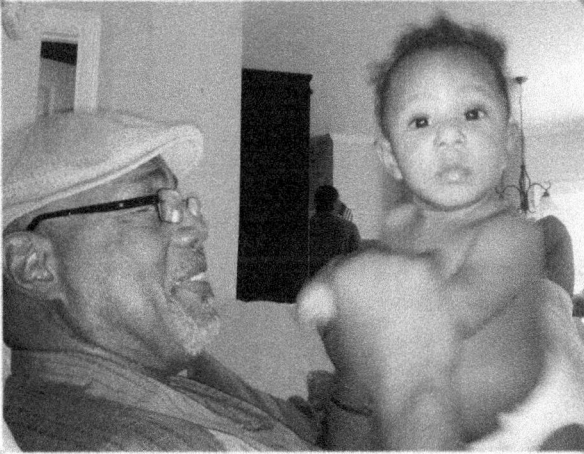

Fred & great grandson, James
Spring 2012

Fred & Joanne Duncan
Fall 2013

Damon, Fred, Joanne, grandchildren,
& great grandchildren
Fall 2013

Damon, Fred, Joanne, & Sabin
Winter 2013

Fred Duncan

Duncan Family at Dinner (Good Times All Around)
Spring 2015

Fred Duncan, Jr.
1971

Fred Duncan

Politics

Listen Up

Donald Trump was elected as the 45th President of the United States, which speaks loudly of the values and beliefs of our fellow countrymen. Certainly, Trump has been consistent: consistently deceitful, racist, sexist, and narcissistic. He consistently proved that he was the inferior candidate. He was also consistent in providing fair-warning of what type of charlatan-in-chief he would be.

But you know America; we invade Iraq when the facts say Al-Qaeda. We solemnly swear we will stabilize the Middle East and since our intervention, the Middle East has been far from stable. We say, "Let's get past racism" but disproportionately imprison people of color. A pastime in our country is to say one thing but do or believe another.

My dad is not bothered by Trump. He recalls a comparable disappointment with the elections of Presidents Nixon and Reagan. My dad and I discussed the possibility of activists becoming more active once President Obama's term expires. I agree that the concept of Obama contributed to a bit of nonchalance. A nonchalance borne from HOPE that because we saw him as one of us, we could loosen our grip and allow our president take the wheel. None of us should trust Trump with the wheel. But hopefully, our distrust of Trump mobilizes a new course of communal action, which is the only source of change in which we can truly believe.

~ *Sabin*

Our Sinking Ship

Have the chickens come home to roost? Lie, after lie, with no semblance of truth, as the band (campaign) played on. Outlandish promises that no human could possibly keep. Plagiarized speeches paraded as authentic. Crowds cheer and the band plays on. When Americans look into the mirror, how many generations can they go back before they too were considered immigrants? As the lifeboats are lowered, the band plays on. The world watches aghast in disbelief! "Is that the S.S. America, listing on the starboard?" Was she disemboweled by some unseen hazard, or was it the crushing weight of political immorality that weakened her structure? Was it her hypocrisy? Was it another betrayal by her elected officials?

Political allegiance has become a cancerous entity with no regard for the good of the country. Men would rather accept a lie than the truth. Unchecked lobbying has altered the direction of our country without any regard for the people. America has been bought-out from under her flag-draped precepts with unaccounted-for money. Yet, the band plays on. Hopefully, Americans can get the bilge of hatred pumped-out and restore sanity to the country's voyage into the future. Maybe she will refuse those thirty pieces of silver, with which billionaires tease. Meanwhile, those of us in steerage have our fingers crossed, wondering will the band play, *Anchors Away* or a funeral dirge?

Fred Duncan

Capable or Captivating?

Finally, the solution to America's ills and the problems that so easily beset her, ladies and gentlemen, the ultimate symbol of what the American mindset endears, and has forsaken religion, the Pledge of Allegiance and even mama's cooking for: the Almighty Dollar. At last, fate has provided a savior, an avatar of sorts. Emerging from the art of the deal, half-truths, innuendos, and out-right lies, America's embodiment of success, our hope for tomorrow: Donald Trump. He's rich, a couple of his kids are cute, his wife is "the shit," and he speaks his mind. Why he even cursed a time or two, on TV! He extols those glory days of our past.

So let us return to those thrilling days of yore, before China's multi-trillion dollar investments, and Saudi Arabian moneyed influence, the Petrodollar, and Fiat Money. Those days before every business call went to India or robots. Alas, we can't return. Not even Trump can turn back time.

America has sold her soul, the Middle Class, for the profit margin and leaving us with those that have and those that do not have. The train has already left with America's Greatness and a chunk of her financial future. Your vote is worth more than smoke and mirrors. When the dust settles, let reality reign. I feel America needs someone in Washington that's capable, rather than just captivating.

The Art of Politics

I first observed the art of living low when I viewed Nixon. Now, -he low road is the current norm in politics. We live in a time when the good of the party trumps the good of the country! Treasonous! But the spin on this treason was Anti-Obamanism, such a sad excuse.

Through the Eyes of a Political Novice

A political novice with even my limited perception can sense the pent-up frustration and hostility towards the current Administration. Including that ultimate scapegoat, Obama, as the President is often derisively referred. The long campaign to steer the country's emotions into that "safe" and o' so familiar harbor of racial fault finding almost guarantees the outcome of the November election. Race has always been a trump card, if you will, in U.S. politics. Too long has America remained locked in myopic refusal, ignoring her Achilles heel, racial injustice. Thus we can expect vignettes such as policemen justifying murder, 'cause Black folks are frightening, and officers flinging hundred pound women around like pizza dough because they feel threatened, to continue. This right-winged atmosphere of racial injustice is tolerably winked at by most of White America. Leaving Blacks abandoned in the streets and the courts - a stain of illegitimacy to our citizenship.

You might conclude that Uncle Sam thinks of Blacks as some

kind of bed wench, only utilized when America needs to get off on his grandeur, such as Olympic gold, or as sacrificial military pawns for excursions into the sovereignty of another country. Blacks are deemed heroes over there, but undeserving side-pieces when it comes to justice here at home.

Meanwhile back in the states, unsubstantiated statistics, outlandish promises, disguise themselves as a political platform. Fault finding, and looking the other way when faced with reality has lead public opinion astray.

The glaring mistake of threatening to disarm America has been pounced on by the political right and married to the disdain for anything Obama thus blinding public opinion to the folly of slick, sentimental speeches and showmanship, which proved to be more "Follywood" than Hollywood. Should be the impulse of entrusting the good of the nation into the hands of a political novice with a majority in Congress at his disposal? Let us not choose sentiment over logic or politics over principle.

Real or Make-Believe?

Just wondering: As beautiful as a diamond is, why is its value so different than other so-called "precious" stones? Is that value real, or make-believe? The popular torn and tattered jeans, what makes them more valuable than a sound pair? We live in a world of make-believe; it starts early, our indoctrination into make-believe. Our children are inundated with seemingly harmless fairy-tales that with at home and certainly, in school. We have no cultural directives; we just imitate what we see in the media. One wonders what those little Jewish children are doing while ours are engrossed in Disney; probably memorizing the Torah. Is it any wonder that those children with a strong cultural influence excel in school and later in life? (I bet they can't do the Quan). It's not just us Blacks, as the majority of news programs have the obligatory "blue--eyed blonde" front and center. America is BS'ing herself, again. Every attractive white girl does not have to be blonde. The really fine ones are not the fairest ones anyway, but that's another issue. Back to real and supposed value, and real vs. make-believe. In this season of hyper make-believe, Presidential election aside, I suggest that we pause and think, is it real or make believe? We blacks cannot afford The American Dream any more than those indigenous Americans at Standing Rock can celebrate Thanksgiving.

Fred Duncan

The Common Cause Charade

Some of the world's religions have turned a blind eye to the deeds of their more unsavory brothers and sisters and their views. That is until they are used as pawns for some seemly greater cause. Politicians are no strangers to utilizing that charade. Suddenly, the highbrow and the lowbrows are brothers again. The highbrow, having gained their objectives after reassuring their lowbrow brothers that they won't be forgotten, are now waving goodbye, rubbing their hands with sanitizer, and disappearing back to their previous perch of self-proclaimed respectability. This election seemed different; the lowbrows wouldn't shut up or go away. The lowbrows are not the polite people of society; they are the gun-toting, tobacco-chewing good ole' boys, who are looking for that wall financed by Mexico, those jobs that were promised, and a revitalized American economy. If not, they may soil the White House lobby with their muddy boots and spew their expletive-laden displeasure toward the president they elected.

Oh! This is going to get interesting folks. Trump won't adhere to the established Republicans, who turned their backs on him during his campaign. There will be some back-peddling and moonwalking by those who opposed him. The questions that remains are: whether America will be great again? Or will America's hallowed symbol, the bald eagle, be dethroned by a buzzard?

What Time Is It?

What time is it? It's time to get real! With all the patriotic attention in the air, the country's bereavement over 9/11, the heightened attention to politics, this election year with its seemingly fatal alternative of candidates, could make a fella become melancholy. Cheer up! The battle is not ours. For a ray of hope returns amid all the sad news, football season! Sadly, even the gridiron is littered with patriotic controversy over long existing ills with long overdue lack of corrections. First amendment be damned! (In my best Jeremiah Wright voice), it's time for football.

Time out! Let the people get real, for a moment, these player protests are but token displays at best. When you are talking about million dollar contracts, public opinion trumps protest. The fans pay for the players' livelihood. So what the fans want, the fans get. We TV football fans understand the protests, but those butts in the seats are the cast of supporters that the players' actions must be in concert with. They call it a sport, but it is really show business, and they expect the players to stay in character for that big money, or bankrolls will grow wings. I know you have your pride and no one can accuse you guys of cooning, just don't languish in the cross-hairs between big business and their "paper." Being right, doesn't pay the bills. Reality does and reality knows no right nor wrong, it just is.

It is a White controlled world from here to the motherland and White folks are about that "paper." That mindset is worldwide and to such depths that it even has most other cultures looking down their noses at America's Blacks. You have made your point and I certainly support that. Don't blow yo' gig, we may not like it, "But it's like that and that's the way it is" (Run DMC).

Self-Inflicted Wounds

The 500 year floods, the 1000 year storms, droughts, and melting ice caps are all warning shots across the bow of public complacency. I, like others, have watched the re-devastation of Louisiana. I have observed the suffering in the shelters and was reminded that suffering has no color. The wrath of Nature may knock at any door, at any time, despite one's economic or racial status. Carbonization of the atmosphere and squandering of natural resources for the good of the company may be culpable. Such indifference has clouded the good of the people, the good of the country and, dare I mention, the good of the planet. Back in the shelters, once stalwart difference in ethnicity and economic status, no longer mattered. Imagine that. The question remains, are we suffering from self-inflicted wounds? To a degree we are.

Bamboozled

Politicians got poor folks out here throwing rocks at each other while neither can safely drink tap water anymore. People who think that a billionaire (Republican or Democrat) is for their best interest are the type that would sit a car seat on the front porch of the White House and think of it as rustic. They may think of themselves as supremacist, I see them as misguided poor folks with a hateful attitude. Having a Beagle and a Bud lite doesn't make one superior. The real White Supremacists wear tailor made suits while fanning the flames of hatred and intolerance among the poor worldwide. They own stock in corporations that make weaponry which ordinary folks can't even afford one share of common stock. They arm Third World countries with rifles rather than rice and instigate conflicts throughout the world to support their business interests. Their patriotism is in offshore tax shelters while they sell hate-blinded Americans patriotism wrapped in flags that were probably made in China. One might say, "Oh those poor darkies, they don't stand a chance." But the reality is that the marginalized minority will have plenty of company in their sufferings with a misdirected poor white majority who thought that wealthy people loved their white skin more than they loved their green money ... told you so, and don't park that pickup on my lawn! Wake up America, the business of America is business; anything less is well, uncivilized.

Fred Duncan

Faith

Listen Up

If memory serves me correctly, I believe Damon and I were together when my dad broke the news. If not, we got the same message.

After having faithfully attended church for nearly a decade as a family, my dad had enough. He was no longer going to attend our church.

One of my take-aways from the ensuing conversation was that did I really think that God, who is Love, was going to send us to Hell because we missed Bible Class? Hell nawl.

My dad's choice to leave our church was the beginning of my spiritual maturity. The beginning of questioning of what is considered "The way" and thinking critically about building "A way" to have a healthy rapport with God.

My dad would raise questions like (these are paraphrases): "If God is no respecter of persons, what makes you think the pastor is closer to God than you are? You are both men." Or, "The people in countries that have never been exposed to Christianity are condemned to Hell because they never heard of Jesus?" Then there was my favorite, "A lot of these attributes we assign to God sound like man's attributes. God created us, knowing we would sin; not that that is an excuse to intentionally do wrong, but do you think it is necessary to put on a lifelong pity party for God to love or forgive us?"

It seems my dad also bore the perspective of how the people who have inflicted the most pain in his life were people who proclaimed to be "On fire for the Lord" and those who have helped him the most were acting through demonstrations of Love without the alleged Jesus pronouncements and endorsements.

My dad's choice was a tipping point in our family life. My mother was deflated. While this is certainly an inadequate attempt to describe her feelings, she was not only disappointed by my father's choice and subsequent non-action, she was concerned about what he was modeling for us. Our attending church as a family was of great value to her. I believe she viewed our membership as glue that held our family together, the nucleus of our social lives, and the bastion of her religious experience. I empathized with her disappointment. Accepting my dad's seemingly abrupt choice was not easy for her. However, it was liberating for me.

For some, my dad's drawing a line of demarcation regarding church attendance was an act of heresy. Indeed in this life, there is much too much time wasted on classifying what is right and what is wrong. With regard to those who disagreed with my dad's choice, I believe their disagreement is an extension of their limited world and spiritual views. I know that my dad's choice liberated me from constricting world and spiritual views. It was a quantum leap in my spiritual growth. By abandoning what many view as the only way to salvation, my dad gave me permission to accept broad humanity, love beyond language and customs, and a stronger rapport with God.

~ Sabin

Fred Duncan

My Greatest Challenge

I do not regret my Christian days or my irrational beliefs during that time. From time to time, I see those former behavioral patterns replicated by others emerging from the cocoons of Christianity and Islam. In times past, upon being questioned, I adamantly defended the faith, even if it took quoting a New Testament's worth of scriptures to impress. I could not bear the thought of "The Deacon" (me) being wrong about my Jesus. What I discovered, was that I was quoting my pastor's opinion more than the Bible. Who was I really trying to convince them or me? If the Bible is your only authoritative reference then you are limiting your growth. However, if you are happy with that, then fine. I've always harbored questions about being the (alleged) cursed seed of Ham. To some, belief rather than knowledge is enough; and that, if nothing else, black and white fundamentalist have in common. They believe according to the Bible that blacks are inferior and too many blacks zealously cosign that lie.

Once I came into the knowledge that there existed other sacred texts besides the Bible and the Koran, the blindness began to slowly abate. Why didn't the Jews whose faith formed a major portion of Christian belief, deify Jesus? Actually, there are several books to expand ones understanding; but that expanded understanding has to be the objective rather than just an acquisition of information to defend the status quo. Once I realized, the Bible was not the final authority, my eyes were opened and are still opening.

A greater discovery was that Black history superseded the religion imposed on my people by our enslavers. To shun Christianity for Islam is to trade the religion of the western slave merchant for the religion of the East African enslaver, but one has to first open their eyes to see. My greatest challenge was admitting to myself that I had been misled, but what American, Black or White, has not? With one foot in the grave, I do not have the patience for fruitless debates on apples when the subject is oranges, those days are past. This is just my opinion with best wishes for increased knowledge, unity and love.

Overzealous & Narrow-Sighted

When organizing some of my books, I ran across one of my old bibles and was reminded of how I once studied, highlighted, underlined and marked specific passages in my quest to be better equipped and better understand "God's Word." My arsenal included my Scofield, my Dak's Annotated, my favorite, the Thompson Chain, and all King James Versions (of course). Ready to shell and bombard any "uncircumcised heathen" that did not share my same belief with a litany of scriptures that either scared them to Hell or out of my all-knowing fanatical presence. Grrr! What I believed to be zeal probably was interpreted as a borderline mental deficiency. If I encountered a sticking point, I would seek the counsel of the pastor or someone else more learned, so that I could be ready for the next encounter with the "unsaved." I deemed myself, a warrior for the Lord.

Oh, I had something for the Mormons that bicycled by, the Muslim at his store, and the Witnesses that came to the door. I was so impressed with my Christian prowess in those little scrimmages that I failed to realize how narrow my perception of the Creator was.

My beliefs were all framed by the King James Version, minus at least eighteen un-canonized books. Yet, the world includes so many people and beliefs. This universe is more than the "Little town of Bethlehem" and the Christian stories that abound from it. There are many opportunities for "Sand-box debates" with those myopic in their conceptions. Having been there and done battle, I have learned to live and let live. Beyond beliefs, there are good people that strive to live an upright and fair life. They are usually less dogmatic and let their lifestyle speak for them. It seems that they have no particular race, religion or social status; they are just decent folk. What was once sufficient, does not cut it in today's more informed society. With more information available, folks are seeking knowledge and truth. No one book has the market cornered. Not even one that was once sacred.

Certain similarities are found throughout all religions, the Golden Rule, being one of them. No doubt, there are Asians who look at our deities and say the Savior doesn't look like that. There are others who question the validity of Christianity, just as Christians question their God's authentication, so it goes. Amazing how one can be so rational about the validity of other doctrines, and yet so irrational about their own beliefs. Been there, done that.

What Kind of God Do We Serve?

The training of my youth sometimes peeks from behind the door of my new found awareness and knowledge of the Creation. Proverbs 22:6 addresses that. So much of my belief has been shaped by the beliefs of grandma and my mother. Dad was always at work. As I matured I begin to realize, that what many adults said exceeded their actions and that many stories shared by adults, believers, both black and white, the Church, and even the country were embellished. Yet, the influence of my upbringing constrains my transition from just believing to knowing.

An integral part of church service was devotion, the time of my greatest enjoyment, which is followed by the messages which were to be applied to life's more pressing issues. Behind the veneer of belief to which so many pay homage, rests a system of control that governs both black and white thinking, with pacification that someday, someway things will be better. We are taught that the Son of God has gone to bat for our sins; he just doesn't look anything like me. Every other race of people serve a deity that looks like them, but our Jesus looks like the enslavers of our ancestors. Does that mean that after all is said and done, when we get to heaven, if you will, I will be an adopted outsider there too?

Would any other race accept a deity that looks like me? The hallowed fervor of black praise seems hollow. For it seems that the emotionless, time censored services of the white church bear the most fruit. Yet, we should only believe and fund or vice versa.

Lord, help me here. My questions seek understanding and unity for a people that need it the most. I may be conflicted by my upbringing, but I won't be content with blind acceptance.

The sanctuary is needed and it takes money to run it. The sanctuary should provide help for the needy, guidance for the lost and spiritual enrichment to the seeker. My belief is that the institution should remain, but the teaching should be updated and made more relevant to the demands of a people whose ancestors gave rise to mankind, Ma'at, and civilization long before slavery and the supremacy system governed this world. After all these years, blind faith was rendered me bent, but the empowerment of awareness keeps me from being broken.

An Afternoon with My Friend

I had the occasion to get out of the house the other day, and visit a friend that had endured one of life's severest trials. I'm glad to say that God has seen him through. We discussed his continuing sobriety and the reunification of his family. We also rapped about the many times God has seen us both through life's hardships and challenges during the forty-plus years that we've known each other. He likes to say that I led him to Christ. A part of me would like to take a bow, but that credit belongs to the account of the Creator, not mine. I am no longer the deacon that I was at that time. Yet, my friend often declares "What the Lord and Savior Jesus Christ" has done in his life. Alas, as a man believes, he is. Knowing what he has endured, I refused to cast any doubt upon his belief, although mine differ, to some degree. Knowing that there are many sacred books utilized by different religions, I continue to question and search for greater clarity of God, Christianity, and the Son of God (Especially, the notion of the Son of God to which I was raised because that notion ranges from a deity to a fabrication of Constantine and the Catholic Church). Nevertheless Christianity remains a staple in the Black community. I look at the Creator as being greater than one religion, one planet, or even this universe.

I have determined that no matter what I do or not believe, mine is not to condemn another's belief, whether I agree or disagree. I see a man's belief as a pillar that supports who he is, so in the spirit of the Golden Rule, I would be wrong to jeopardize his stability with my belief. More to my point, everyone has the right to believe what they choose and mine is not to force mine upon them. Therefore, I disapprove of religious escapades as the Crusades as much as I disapprove of these so-called jihadists who use religion as an excuse to murder and maim is unleashing evil to promote good. Such logic is frightening and unethical.

Mankind has made competition a means of existence; but I feel that humanity serves the greater good. What one practices is truer than what one says. Competition has led men to the threshold of non-existence. Humanity is a much better option. For we are brothers, bound by one blood, with one destiny for the body (and who knows of the spirit) - the March to the grave. So why must we fight our way to that common destiny in some effort to say, "I'm better than you, or any man." I am afraid that men have made fools of themselves, thinking that one is any more worthy than another. History has proven that none are above the corruption of power, not one.

Fred Duncan

More than One Way

It amazes me, although it shouldn't, that whenever I raise a question about the Church, or Christianity, some immediately conclude that I'm refuting the existence of God or a Creative Consciousness. That is not the case. Even a beginner of the faith would have to but read Saint Thomas Aquinas to cement that belief with logic. What a person learns about his Maker is an ongoing process, with many questions to be answered along the path. The well-trodden path doesn't make it "The way," but merely a way, that many have tread. A perspective that might be considered is Dr. Jeremiah Wright lesson on Sibling Rivalry. Considering the options, makes sense to me. The eternity of one's spirit and soul is too important to me to just rest on one point of view. Myopic? Hardly.

Not Yet

Believing in the eternity of the spirit, I feel that God has an even greater array of magnificence, beyond what our bodily encapsulated spirit has yet to behold. Therefore, disrobing my soul of death's apprehension, mortality no longer holds the sway it once held. I'm strengthened by the words of that sacred few, who having returned from death's threshold and having peeked at the grandeur beyond, reluctantly returned, summoned by the Creator, "Not yet."

Praise God

There awaits a special blessing for the spirit of all brethren, especially those conscious of the Master. Some used to say that the spirit fell or was just bearing witness to itself, but whatever you call it - it can be recognized as a spontaneous expression of appreciation, an impromptu celebration of praise, a pervasive vibration of joy, and magnanimity among the people. I have observed this phenomenon both in barefoot indigenous forest dwellers and in proper folks worshipping in mega-churches. Logic can't comprehend that type of emotion until one has no place to turn, all options have been exhausted, and grace or whatever you call it, arises unseen to make a way where you saw none. That's when one knows fa' sho' and can proclaim, "My help comes from the Creator, my Comforter."

I have not been "Called" as my friend, Reverend Fishing Buddy, has and "Filled with" or "Saved" remain grey areas, as many claiming the loftier levels have proven to be subject to the same imperfections as the rest of us, all of those things are of little consequence at the moment of enlightenment. I know or recognize that occasionally there is a breakout of passionate celebration of joy and to me it bespeaks of the presence of the Holy Spirit.

Love, peace, and harmony, chillun (that's Mississippian, for children)!

Epilogue

Listen Up

Sometimes in order to provide a correct and conclusive ending, one must first go back to the beginning. As a father, a husband, an uncle, a brother, and even a grandfather, all that I am and yet to become, I owe to my father. Fred Lee Duncan, Jr.

A mere few months after the rebellion of 1967 on March 3, 1968, my physical birth into this realm became a reality. Yet it was not until the age of 9 that I felt a true sense of being born.

This birth occurred at McKenney Elementary School, located at Pembroke and Burt Road on Detroit's Northwest side. It was there that I was introduced to using my mind and my hands to complete a set of tasks. It was there that I gain the perspective of how a series of tasks can ultimately result in the completion of a project. When assigned the project by my third grade teacher, I remember feeling completely overwhelmed because this assignment could not be completed in one evening. Overwhelmed by the prospect of creating a project that demonstrated my grasp of the material while also being aesthetically captivating. Overwhelmed because I thought I had to do it alone.

I was not alone. My dad understood my feelings and dove-in with life lessons that continue to resonate. Today, I am one of the more prolific professionals in my field of urban development. Others celebrate my achievements without knowing my strategy, my ambition, and my work ethic were launched through that third grade project.

According to most dictionary meanings: A tanyard is an enclosure where the tanning of leather is carried out. Ye Olde Tanyard is the funny name that branded my school project and ultimately my view of myself and what I could accomplish. Using a box, some construction paper, fuzzy wire and magic markers, my dad helped me to construct a tanyard setting that depicted various figures carrying-out a wide range of duties. An already great project grew to the heights of causing astonishment once my dad and I remained in the classroom after school hours to complete construction.

I don't recall sleeping at all that night. I was afraid that my project was a little too over-the-top and that it would somehow be looked-down upon by my peers and our teacher. I remember walking into the classroom and heading toward the rear, where all the projects were located - only to find that Ye Olde Tanyard was not among the others. It was carefully displayed at the front of the class. The teacher had selected it as a as a model of what an excellent project resembles.

With a single elementary school project, my dad introduced me to pride and the work that produces it. He probably doesn't recall the specificity of that elementary school project that took place 40 years ago; but I'm sure he remembers the lesson of teaching us to see beyond what is most visible or what is readily accessible. I am sure he remembers instilling in us the vision to see a broader, grander perspective. A vision further beyond than what he himself had modeled for us.

"There is a whole world that exists beyond 8-Mile Rd," he would often say in reference to the city border near our home. Yet for an elementary school-aged boy in Detroit, the foundation for building a world beyond 8-Mile came in the form of Ye Olde Tanyard.

~ Damon

Fred Duncan

About the Authors

Fred Duncan, Jr., was born in Hattiesburg, Mississippi, came of age in Flint, MI, and raised his family in Detroit. He is a retiree of Ford Motor Company where he began on the assembly line and ended as skilled-trade electrician. He is the loving husband of Joanne, proud father of Damon (Mary) and Sabin (Ramona), extra proud grandfather or Ryan, David, Damon II, Dominique, Sanaa and Seylon, and super proud great-grandfather of Ce'Asia, Ryan, Jr., James, Aubrey, Austin, and Jayde.

Sabin Prentis Duncan is a husband, father, educator, native Detroiter, lover of authentic hip-hop, and Fred's youngest son. He is owner of Fielding Books and the author of *Assuming Hurts*, *Reflections from the Frontline*, and co-author of *Four Floors*. He can be reached at www.sabinprentis.com.

www.ingramcontent.com/pod-product-compliance
Lightning Source LLC
Chambersburg PA
CBHW021213020426
42331CB00003B/335